Dream BIG
American Idol SUPERSTARS

Kris Allen

David Archuleta

Kelly Clarkson

David Cook

Chris Daughtry

Jennifer Hudson

Adam Lambert

Kellie Pickler

Jordin Sparks

Carrie Underwood

Elliott Yamin

American Idol Profiles Index:
Top Finalists from Seasons 1 to 7
(82 Contestants)

Insights Into American Idol

Kelly Clarkson

Gail Snyder

Mason Crest Publishers

Produced by 21st Century Publishing and Communications, Inc.

MASON CREST PUBLISHERS INC.
370 Reed Road
Broomall, Pennsylvania 19008
(866) MCP-BOOK (toll free)
www.masoncrest.com

Printed in the United States of America.

First Printing

9 8 7 6 5 4 3 2 1

Library of Congress Cataloging-in-Publication Data

Snyder, Gail.
    Kelly Clarkson / Gail Snyder.
        p. cm. — (Dream big: American Idol superstars)
    Includes bibliographical references and index.
    ISBN 978-1-4222-1506-7 (hardback : alk. paper)
    ISBN 978-1-4222-1604-0 (pbk. : alk. paper)
    1. Clarkson, Kelly, 1982–   —Juvenile literature. 2. Singers—United States—
Biography—Juvenile literature. I. Title.
    ML3930.C523S69 2010
    782.42164092—dc22
        [B]   2009021195

CONTENTS

American Idol TIMELINE

October 5, 2001

Pop Idol, a TV reality show created by Simon Fuller, debuts in the United Kingdom and becomes a smash hit.

Fall 2001

Based on the success of *Pop Idol*, and after initially rejecting the concept, FOX Network agrees to buy *American Idol*, a national talent competition and TV reality show.

Spring 2002

Auditions for *American Idol* Season 1 are held in New York City, Los Angeles, Chicago, Dallas, Miami, Atlanta, and Seattle.

January 21, 2003

American Idol Season 2 premieres without Brian Dunkleman, leaving Ryan Seacrest as the sole host.

May 21, 2003

- *American Idol* Season 2 finale airs.
- Ruben Studdard narrowly wins and Clay Aiken is the runner-up.
- Runner-up Clay Aiken goes on to become extremely successful both critically and commercially.

January 19, 2004

American Idol Season 3 premieres.

2001   2002   2003   2004

June 11, 2002

American Idol Season 1 premieres on FOX Network, with Simon Cowell, Paula Abdul, and Randy Jackson as the judges, and Ryan Seacrest and Brian Dunkleman as the co-hosts.

September 4, 2002

- *American Idol* Season 1 finale airs.
- Kelly Clarkson wins and Justin Guarini is the runner-up.
- Kelly Clarkson goes on to become the most successful Idol winner and a superstar in the music industry.

Fall 2002

Auditions for *American Idol* Season 2 are held in New York City, Los Angeles, Miami, Detroit, Nashville, and Austin.

January 27, 2004

William Hung's audition is aired and his humble response to Simon Cowell's scathing criticism make William the most famous American Idol non-qualifier and earn him record deals and a cult-like following.

April 21, 2004

Jennifer Hudson is voted off the show in 7th place, and goes on to win the role of Effie in *Dreamgirls*, for which she wins an Academy Award, a Golden Globe Award, and a Grammy Award.

May 26, 2004

- *American Idol* Season 3 finale airs with 65 million viewers casting their votes.
- Fantasia Barrino is crowned the winner and Diana DeGarmo is the runner-up.
- Fantasia soon becomes the first artist in the history of Billboard to debut at number one with her first single.

May 10, 2006

Chris Daughtry is voted off the show in 4th place, and soon after forms the band, Daughtry, and releases its debut album, which becomes number one on the charts, wins many awards, and finds huge commercial success.

April 26, 2006

Kellie Pickler is voted off the show in 6th place, and soon releases her debut album, which rockets to number one on the Billboard Top Country Album chart.

January 17, 2006

American Idol Season 5 premieres and for the first time airs in high definition.

May 24, 2006

- *American Idol* Season 5 finale airs.
- Taylor Hicks is the winner and Katharine McPhee the runner-up.
- Elliot Yamin, the second runner-up, goes on to release his debut album, which goes gold.

January 16, 2007

American Idol Season 6 premieres.

April 2007

The *American Idol* Songwriting Contest is announced.

January 15, 2008

American Idol Season 7 airs with a four-hour two-day premiere.

April 9, 2008

Idol Gives Back returns for its second year.

May 21, 2008

- *American Idol* Season 7 finale airs.
- David Cook wins with 54.6 million votes and David Archuleta is the runner-up with 42.9 million votes.
- Both Davids go on to tremendous post-Idol success with successful albums and singles.

2005   2006   2007   2008   2009

May 25, 2005

- *American Idol* Season 4 finale airs.
- Carrie Underwood wins and Bo Bice is the runner-up.
- Carrie goes on to become one of the most successful Idol winners, selling millions of albums and winning scores of major awards.

January 18, 2005

- *American Idol* Season 4 premieres.
- Some rules change:
  - The age limit is raised from 24 to 28.
  - The semi-final competition is separated by gender up until the 12 finalists.

April 24–25, 2007

American Idol Gives Back, a charitable campaign to raise money for underprivileged children worldwide, airs, and raises more than $70 million.

May 23, 2007

- *American Idol* Season 6 finale airs.
- Jordin Sparks wins with 74 million votes and Blake Lewis is the runner-up.
- Jordin goes on to join Kelly Clarkson and Carrie Underwood in the ranks of highly successful post-Idol recording artists.

January 13, 2009

American Idol Season 8 premieres adding Kara DioGuardi as a fourth judge.

February 14, 2009

The American Idol Experience, a theme park attraction, officially opens at Disney's Hollywood Studio in Florida.

May 20, 2009

- *American Idol* Season 8 finale airs.
- Kris Allen unexpectedly wins and Adam Lambert is the runner-up.
- Almost 100 million people voted in the season 8 finale.

Kelly Clarkson may have been shocked to win two Grammy Awards in 2006, but she had been planning what song to sing at the ceremonies since she was a teenager in Texas. The first *American Idol* winner to win a Grammy, Kelly was honored for her album *Breakaway* and her single "Since U Been Gone."

1

Double Grammy Winner!

When Kelly Clarkson was 16, she was already thinking about the Grammy Awards. She told her girlfriend Ashley what she would sing when she made it to the biggest award ceremony in the recording arts. It would be "Because of You," a song she had just written whose lyrics describe the raw emotions Kelly experienced after her parents divorced.

Eight years later, on February 8, 2006, when Kelly attended the 48th Grammy Awards, she brought along Ashley to hear her sing her powerful **ballad** "Because of You," exactly as she said she would. The song was one of the smash hits from Kelly's second album, *Breakaway*, which had been nominated for Best Pop Vocal Album. Kelly was nominated for Best Female Pop Vocal Performance for her performance on another song from the album, "Since U Been Gone."

As Ashley looked on in the audience, Kelly was the picture of the calm superstar as she performed, accompanied by a drummer, a string section, and a pianist. Her calm appearance faded later that evening when rhythm and blues superstar Stevie Wonder declared Kelly winner of the Grammy for Best Female Pop Vocal Performance.

WHAT ARE THE GRAMMY AWARDS?

Kelly Clarkson was the first *American Idol* winner to capture a Grammy Award—actually two of them in the same year. The nationally televised Grammy Awards show, which is always held in February in Los Angeles, is produced by the National Academy of Recording Arts & Sciences. The show recognizes recording artists in more than 100 categories—everything from classical music to hip-hop.

Winners are presented with an award that looks like an old gramophone, a machine for playing records that dates back to the 1800s. What sets the Grammys apart from other awards is that the winners are determined by other artists in the recording industry and not by the public or through album sales. Winners are selected by voting members of the academy, who have all been associated with at least six commercially released tracks, perhaps as vocalists, producers, conductors, or arrangers.

Crying Time Again

She later told an interviewer that as she walked toward the stage to receive the honor she felt like a shaky and excited 12-year-old who could not control her tears of happiness. As she accepted her first Grammy, Kelly said,

Kelly tearfully accepts the 2006 Grammy Award for Best Female Pop Vocal Performance for "Since U Been Gone." She was very emotional after winning over Mariah Carey and three other more experienced artists. Kelly had also cried tears of joy when she was named the first American Idol in 2002.

> **❝I'm sorry I'm crying again on national television. You have no idea what this means to me.❞**

The scene was a familiar one to Kelly's fans who remembered that she also cried after she was voted winner of *American Idol* during the television series' first season in 2002. And now, just four years later, she had become the first *Idol* winner to win a Grammy Award—the highest tribute a recording artist may receive.

Certainly, Kelly was surprised by her win, which was considered something of an upset. Many recording industry insiders predicted Mariah Carey would win. Carey had staged a **comeback** that year and was the sentimental favorite. Also up for the award were Sheryl Crow, Gwen Stefani, and Bonnie Raitt—women who had been honing their craft a lot longer than Kelly.

Beating the Beatle

The competition was also fierce for the second Grammy Award for which Kelly was nominated, Best Pop Vocal Album. In addition to

Kelly puts her heart into her rendition of "Because of You" at the 48th annual Grammy Awards. For her, the best part of the night was the chance to perform for an audience filled with singing stars and members of the music industry whom she had always admired.

Crow and Stefani, the other formidable nominees were former Beatle Paul McCartney and Fiona Apple. When Kelly was named winner of that Grammy she regained her composure. She gushed,

> **❝I don't know what is going on, but thank you Jesus and God. I'm so proud of myself for not crying [this time].❞**

That night, during her acceptance speeches, an excited Kelly also thanked her mother, her record label, her manager, and her friend Ashley. She did not mention *American Idol*, which left some commentators wondering whether Kelly was trying to put her *Idol* days behind her. Asked about it later, Kelly said that was not so. She pointed out that she had also forgotten to thank her father and stepfather. She said, "I forgot. You forget. Especially since the first time I was bawling."

Humbled to Perform

For Kelly, the highlight of the evening was the chance to perform in front of an audience that included such stars as McCartney and Raitt as well as Steven Tyler and Madonna, whom she met that night.

Kelly was thunderstruck that she won, noting that some of her guy friends who were also Beatles fans were not going to be happy with her. In her eyes, though, she was a winner long before she received the first award. She was a success the moment she went on stage and lived the fantasy she had been picturing since she was a little girl in Burleson, Texas, watching the Grammy Awards show on television and singing songs from the show during commercial breaks. She said,

> **❝To be able to perform for people in the industry where you wanted to be for people you looked up to since you were little, that's the highest.❞**

Kelly has always been proud of her small-town Texas roots. Although her family didn't have much money and went through the upheaval of divorce, Kelly stayed grounded. She was a good student and realized early on she wanted to be a professional singer.

2

Proud Texan

Kelly comes by her simple, unaffected country-girl image honestly. Less than 30,000 people live in her hometown of Burleson, which is about 10 miles south of Fort Worth, a city of more than 1 million people. Burleson is a town where friendships matter, NASCAR racing is hot, and simple pleasures like bowling and going to the movies are appreciated.

As the youngest of three children, Kelly liked to entertain her parents, Steve and Jeanne Clarkson, and siblings, Alyssa and Jason, by belting out upbeat Disney songs from her favorite movies. But her early life did not resemble a Disney movie.

Kelly Brianne Clarkson was born April 24, 1982, to a mother who taught first grade and a father who sold automobiles. Their marriage broke up when Kelly was six years old. Kelly was devastated; in one blow she lost her father as well as her brother and sister, who moved in with relatives in other states. Kelly remained with her mother, and eventually, her mother's second husband, Jimmy Taylor, who stepped in to fill her father's role. The family never had a lot of money.

Champion Sleeper

Kelly was a tomboy who didn't care for dresses and girly things. In fact, as a toddler she liked to run around with no clothes on. And her casual attitude about clothes and her tendency to sleep late sometimes led to her wearing pajamas to school. Her mother recalled,

> **[Kelly] was easy to raise, except for having to get her up in the morning to go to school. When they say she sometimes went [to school] in her pajamas, they mean it. The alarm clock would be blasting right beside her head, and she didn't hear a thing. The house could have fallen apart and she'd still be sleeping.**

Kelly was a good student who joined her middle school choir at the urging of a teacher who heard her singing in the hall. Kelly first realized that she wanted to be a professional singer at age 13 when she got the opportunity to sing her first solo in front of other students.

She also appeared as a lead in several high school musicals. However, on one occasion when the lead went to someone else, Kelly briefly worried that she had been passed over because she weighed too much. She began to focus too much on what she ate, became **bulimic**, and was embarrassed when a male friend called her out on it. She stopped immediately.

Expressing Herself

Kelly's friend Ashley bought her a **karaoke** machine, which she placed in Kelly's closet, dubbing it "Kelly's recording studio." The two would sit in the closet while Kelly sang the songs of her favorite artists—people like Mariah Carey, Steven Tyler, Whitney Houston, and Aretha Franklin.

Kelly has always admired Aretha Franklin, a rhythm and blues singer known as Lady Soul. Kelly sang "Respect," one of Aretha's signature songs, three times during the *Idol* competition. So Kelly was doubly thrilled when she later learned that Aretha is also one of her fans.

COUNTING ARETHA AMONG HER FANS

One of Kelly's greatest thrills was to find out that Aretha Franklin, a rhythm and blues singer she had admired since she was a little girl, is one of her fans. "To know someone you've looked up to for years likes your stuff is amazing," Kelly said.

During the *American Idol* competition, Kelly sang one of her favorite Aretha songs, "Respect," on three occasions because she believed the song would showcase her own ability to be soulful and to demonstrate the power she could bring to her singing.

Aretha was the first woman to be inducted into the Rock 'n' Roll Hall of Fame and has had more top 40 singles than any other female recording artist. Perhaps more impressively, she has had hit songs in four different decades. The Grammy Award–winning artist got her musical start as a child singing in her clergyman father's church in Detroit. Her most recent honor was singing at the inauguration of Barack Obama in January 2009.

Kelly also began writing songs using emotions she rarely let show as inspiration for her lyrics. At 15 she turned down a recording contract. Still, she knew where she was heading. She said,

> **Friends at school were nervous because they didn't know what they wanted to do with the rest of their lives, but I had a special peaceful feeling inside because I knew. I knew that I would make a living at this since a seventh-grade assembly, when I was about to go out and sing a Mariah Carey song in front of the whole town. Other singers were throwing up out of fear but I wasn't afraid at all. Singing just seemed like a natural thing.**

A Rough Start

After her high school graduation in 2000, Kelly and a friend headed to California to launch their musical careers. But things

Kelly's soulful style began as she practiced singing with a karaoke machine that a friend bought her. At the same time, she began writing songs inspired by her life experiences. Although Kelly was only a teenager, a singing career seemed like the most natural thing in the world to her.

did not go as smoothly as they hoped, especially for Kelly. After a series of bad breaks that included an apartment fire, Kelly headed home thinking that her dream of being a famous singer would have to be deferred.

Back in Texas Kelly reconnected with a high school friend named Jessica whose mother heard about a new television show called *American Idol*. Jessica's mother encouraged Kelly to audition. Jessica also thought this was a good idea and, when Kelly was slow to embrace it herself, Jessica filled out the application for her.

Kelly shows her confidence in an appearance on *American Idol*. She was comfortable with herself and her powerful singing style. Her personality and clear talent made it seem easy for her to make it to the top 30 and then the top 10 contestants.

3

Hands Down, the Best Competitor

Kelly didn't give up easily on her dream of being a pop star. When her apartment building in Los Angeles burned, she escaped with only a pair of red pajamas and the flip-flops on her feet. She spent a short time living in her car before realizing she had little choice but to head back to Texas.

Back home, she found a part-time job promoting Red Bull energy drinks, handing out free samples. On the day she auditioned for *American Idol*, she arrived at the Wyndham Anatole Hotel in Dallas to audition knowing that she had to be at work afterwards.

Aware of her own habit of sleeping through the alarm clock, Kelly had stayed awake all night, arriving at the hotel at daybreak to wait with the other hopefuls for her chance to step before the judges.

As with the 10,000 other people who auditioned in Los Angeles, Seattle, New York, Atlanta, Miami, Hollywood, and Dallas, she didn't know what to expect because *American Idol* was a new reality television show. Kelly recalls,

> **66 We didn't know it was a TV show until the third audition. We didn't know what we were getting into. . . . I just thought it was an audition. And they said you get paid. I was like, 'Man, I need electricity, so I will do it.' 99**

Making It Look Easy

One thing was clear to her that first day as she watched nine other women who auditioned before her come out crying: the judges could be brutal.

But, as contestant No. 2311, Kelly sang "At Last," an Etta James song, for judges Randy Jackson, Simon Cowell, and Paul Abdul. As she performed, Randy subtly nodded his head yes and a big smile played over Paula's face. Simon's expression was impossible to read, but all three judges voted to let Kelly continue. Showing just how comfortable she was, Kelly even offered to change places with Randy, taking his judging chair while Randy auditioned for her. Kelly said, "I was so happy because the British man didn't make me cry."

The British man was Simon, who along with Simon Fuller of 19 Entertainment, brought the *American Idol* concept to America after it caught on in Great Britain under the name *Pop Idol*. The new program hit the American airwaves as a summer replacement show in June 2002. It ran twice a week for 13 weeks on the Fox network. What made *American Idol* different was that people watching the show at home were given opportunities to vote for their favorite singers. Based on the audience vote, the singer scoring the fewest votes would be eliminated from the show each week until a winner was determined.

In addition to the judges, the first season featured two co-hosts, Ryan Seacrest, an influential radio talk show host in Los Angeles

Kelly appears before the *Idol* judges as contestant number 2311 during her audition in Dallas. At the time, *Idol* was so new, she didn't know she was trying out for a reality show. She was just trying to make money to pay the rent.

who had branched out to television, and Brian Dunkleman, a stand-up comic. Ryan and Brian would interview the singers after they performed to add their perspectives to the comments made by the three judges. While Ryan continued on with the show, Brian spent only one season on the program, leaving to pursue an acting career.

Making the Top 10

Kelly made the cut when the audition pool was reduced to 30 and finally to the 10 contestants who would compete on the show. The

SITTING IN THE JUDGES' SEATS

Season one contestants had no idea what the judges of the competition would be like but quickly learned that Randy, Simon, and Paula were each blessed with unique talents and personalities.

Randy, who looks like a big teddy bear, is the only African American on the panel. The New Orleans native favors colorful slang like calling people "dawg" and has years of experience signing musical talent for major record labels and producing gold and platinum record albums. He has worked with Madonna and Destiny's Child.

Simon, whom the British press dubbed "Mr. Nasty," proved himself adept at signing hit-making recording stars in Great Britain before arriving in the U.S. to launch *American Idol*. His blunt comments about the contestants provide dramatic tension.

Paula is a Grammy Award–winning performance artist and humanizing force on the *Idol* judges panel. Having sold more than 30 million of her own records, Paula understands more than anyone what it takes to perform for an audience of critics.

other singers on season one besides Kelly were Justin Guarini, Nikki McKibbin, Tamyra Gray, Ryan Starr, Jim Verraros, A.J. Gil, Christina Christian, EJay Day, and R.J. Helton. All of them had much in common: they were all between the ages of 16 and 24, none had signed record contracts or retained promoters, and all wanted to go home with the $1 million recording deal promised by the show's producers.

In addition to performing different numbers together on the program, all the *American Idol* finalists were required to live together in a large mansion in Los Angeles. They ended up spending very little time there, however. Instead, their lives were totally devoted to working around the clock to learn their songs and **choreography** and fulfill promotional demands. Kelly learned to function with just a few hours of sleep each night. Mostly, she loved the opportunity to perform. In Kelly's view, season one of *American Idol* was more innocent than the seasons that followed. She remembered,

"Our show was so different from how it is now. Now there's all this pressure . . . but we were just a bunch of kids that wanted to make music—it was almost like performing in bars for 10 people, like I used to."

Just Like Céline

Kelly was the only contestant who never ended up in the bottom three of the voting; perhaps the worst thing Simon ever said to Kelly was that he didn't remember her from some of her earlier performances.

American Idol judges Simon Cowell (left), Paula Abdul, and Randy Jackson pose with host Ryan Seacrest (center). On the show, each judge has a clear personality. Simon can be sarcastic, Randy is more laid back, and Paula is warm and encouraging to most contestants.

The top 10 finalists from *Idol* season one were fierce competitors on the show. Between shows, they lived together in a big mansion. They didn't spend much time there sleeping, though. Their exhausting schedules included many song and dance rehearsals and promotional appearances.

The greatest compliment he offered Kelly came when she performed Céline Dion's "I Surrender" during the show devoted to music from the 1990s. Simon and Randy both acknowledged that Kelly presented the song well, even though her voice was so strained and tired she could barely talk. Nonetheless, Simon said,

❝I think you just put yourself in the same league as Céline and Mariah Carey.❞

Paula really captured Kelly's personality in a nutshell when she told her,

> **We feel like we know you. You are dorky, you are adorable, and you know what, I just love you and your personality, and your voice is unbelievable.**

Kelly seems assured as she waits for the judges' comments after an *Idol* performance. Instead of being critical, Simon praised Kelly and put her on a par with Céline Dion and Mariah Carey. Paula called Kelly adorable and agreed with Randy that her voice was amazing.

The top three contestants in *Idol*'s first season were Nikki McKibbin (left), Kelly, and Justin Guarini. After Nikki was eliminated, the battle was on between Kelly and Justin. When Kelly won, both Nikki and Justin were happy for her. They both agreed that the audience had made the right decision.

By late August the competition was down to just three singers—Nikki, a 23-year-old single mom from Grand Prairie, Texas; Justin, a 23-year-old singer from Pennsylvania who often performed at weddings and **bar mitzvahs**, and Kelly. When Nikki was eliminated in late August, it came down to a duel between Justin and Kelly, both of whom had many fans. Justin and Kelly went head-to-head, each singing two songs written specifically for the show: "A Moment Like This" and "Before Your Love." In addition, both were allowed to choose another song that would showcase their talents. Justin chose "Get Here" by pop singer Brenda Russell and Kelly reached back to her old favorite, "Respect."

In the audience were many celebrities who were fans of the show; among them were singer Natalie Cole and comedian Ray Romano. When the more than 15 million votes were counted, Kelly won with a margin of 58 percent. Simon commented that he thought the public had chosen well. He said, "She was head and shoulders above the other guy. No competition." Justin appeared genuinely happy for Kelly when he learned that she won. Nikki was also happy with the audience's decision. She said, "She has obviously been the crowd favorite and she just deserves every stitch of everything she is receiving."

WHATEVER HAPPENED TO JUSTIN?

The first season of *American Idol* ended dramatically with a head-to-head competition between powerhouse Kelly and curly-haired Justin Guarini, who ultimately came in second. Justin and Kelly later appeared in one film together, *From Justin to Kelly*, and as a direct result of being on *American Idol* Justin was also signed to a record contract with RCA. The record company produced one album with the young aspiring artist, the self-titled *Justin Guarini*. Following that album, Justin parted company with RCA but has produced two well-received albums on his own.

Justin was born Justin Eldrin Bell in Columbus, Georgia. He grew up in the home of his mother and stepfather in Doylestown, Pennsylvania. He was a member of boys' choirs at an early age and attended the same high school as pop star Pink.

In addition to performing and recording, Justin has appeared in the movie *Fast Girl* and the yet-to-be released movie *Mafioso II*. He has performed on several TV shows relating to *American Idol*, including *Idol Tonight* and *Idol Wrap*. He has also appeared on the music television show *Gone Country*.

Surprised to Win

During the final moment of the results show, Kelly sang "A Moment Like This" one more time. As she sang, her voice strong despite her obvious effort to hold her tears in check, confetti floated down from the ceiling. Kelly's mom could be seen in the audience with tears streaming down her cheeks. Kelly would say later that she really hadn't expected to win. She merely hoped that she would attract some attention to herself that would get her career started.

One music critic later wrote about her final performance:

> **❝Clarkson sang the dickens out of the heroically sappy 'Moment Like This' and began her ascent from Burleson, Texas, cocktail waitress to Grammy winner.❞**

Kelly is the center of a group hug by the top 10 contestants after being crowned the first *American Idol*. Kelly's post-*Idol* success drew more interest in the show, which in turn showcased more bright stars of the future. Even *Idol* contestants who have not won often go on to music success.

As for Kelly, she was thinking to herself:

"I remember being on stage that night and saying to myself, 'I don't want to put out a CD right away. I want to make sure I love everything I do. . . . Now that people voted for me, I'm going to have this opportunity.' I kept thinking to myself, 'Just don't blow it.'"

IDOL STARS NOMINATED FOR GRAMMYS

Although Kelly was the first *Idol* contes-tant to snare a Grammy, she was not the last, proving that the television program shines the spotlight on truly attention-deserving individuals capable of competing with artists who got their starts more conventionally.

The year after Kelly won her first Grammys, Carrie Underwood, winner of *American Idol* season four, won Best Female County Vocal Performance for "Jesus, Take the Wheel" as well as Best New Artist. The following year, Carrie was chosen for the Grammy for Best Female Country Vocal Performance for "Before He Cheats" and took home another in 2009 for Best Female County Vocal Solo for "Last Name."

Jennifer Hudson, a top 10 finalist in season three, was awarded a Grammy for Best Rhythm and Blues Album for her debut CD, *Jennifer Hudson*, in 2009.

Other *Idol* stars who have received nominations but have yet to win include Fantasia Barrino, winner of *Idol* season three; and Chris Daughtry and Mandisa, both contestants and top 10 finalists from season five.

Indeed, as Kelly's career took off she would find herself repeatedly standing up to powerful and experienced record executives in order to assert creative control over her music. She would also vow never to forget her childhood friends or the person she was at her core. One of the first big-ticket purchases she made was a classic Corvette sports car which she gave to her friend Jessica—the girl who suggested that Kelly audition for *American Idol*.

After Kelly's *Idol* win, she performed in concerts and released a chart-topping single. She was not only writing and recording her own songs but also finding her own sound. Fans spread the word about her talent, and soon award nominations came streaming in.

4

Finding Her Own Sound

Soon after *American Idol*'s first season finale, the producers released Kelly's version of "A Moment Like This" as a single. The song quickly caught fire with the public. Fans snapped up 236,000 copies the first week alone, proving that *American Idol* was more than just a television show—it had the power to sell records, too.

Almost from the start Kelly began receiving award nominations. Four months after the release of "A Moment Like This" in 2002, she was nominated for an American Music Award for Favorite Pop-Rock Artist. The award went to Ashanti but it was clear that Kelly's talent was getting noticed. Shortly thereafter, when Kelly's first album, *Thankful*, debuted, it earned her first Grammy Award nomination for Best Female Pop Vocal for the single "Miss Independent." Again, Kelly did not win but she was clearly playing with the big boys—including legendary music hit-maker Clive Davis, who produced *Thankful*.

As the name of her first album would indicate, Kelly really did have a lot for which to be grateful and proud. *Thankful* contained four songs on which Kelly had been credited as writer: "Miss Independent," "The Trouble with Love Is," "You Thought Wrong," and the title track, "Thankful." "Miss Independent" was originally intended to be performed by Christina Aguilera, who is one of its co-authors, but she decided not to finish the song. Kelly and Rhett Lawrence finalized the lyrics and were rewarded with an ASCAP Pop Music Award for the song in 2004. ASCAP, which stands for American Society of Composers, Authors, and Publishers, is an organization of songwriters and music publishers. Receiving an award from other songwriters so early in her career was a big moment for Kelly.

Thankful Goes Platinum

Another cut on the album, "You Thought Wrong," featured a duet in which Kelly performed with Tamyra Gray, who finished fourth on *Idol*'s first season. The album soon reached **platinum** status. Still, some critics found fault with it because they felt it failed to provide Kelly with a distinctive sound of her own. A reviewer from *Rolling Stone* wrote,

> **❝The album's producers jam Clarkson into the stilettos of MTV sexpots ranging from Faith Hill ("Low") to Vanessa Carlton ("Just Missed the Train") to Christina Aguilera ("Miss Independent"). Her high notes are sweet and pillowy, her growl is bone-shaking and sexy, and her midrange is amazingly confident for a pop posy whose career is tied for eternity to the**

whims of her *American Idol* overlords. *Thankful* is testament to marketable young ladies with more talent than artistic freedom. ”

And a reporter for *USA Today* wrote, "I doubt that Clarkson could have released a debut album that sounds more calculated or less original than *Thankful*."

Kelly agreed that the album failed to fully explore her talent. She said, "No one really knew me coming off *American Idol*, no one really knew what to do with me, except for me."

During *Idol*'s season two finale, runner-up Clay Aiken (left) and winner Ruben Studdard congratulate Kelly on her album *Thankful* going platinum. Although Kelly was thrilled at the record's sales, she agreed with critics that the album didn't show off her talent to her best advantage.

Kelly and Justin, her runner-up, appeared in the 2003 movie *From Justin to Kelly*. Neither had acting experience, and the critically panned movie did nothing to advance their careers. Fortunately Kelly soon began a whirlwind tour, where she reached thousands of adoring fans.

GOT MILK?

In keeping with her wholesome image, in 2005 Kelly joined about 250 celebrities in participating in a famous advertising campaign titled "Got Milk?" The campaign depicts celebrities posing with "milk mustaches," conveying the idea that drinking milk is hip enough that even celebrities proudly do it.

Kelly said,

"It's a cool thing to be part of the ["Got Milk?"] campaign. My mom always told me to drink milk growing up because it's good for energy and stuff, especially when you're growing . . . it's good for your bones."

Movie with Justin

Another project that failed to explore her talent would turn out to be Kelly's most embarrassing career misstep. *American Idol* obligated Kelly and *Idol* runner-up Justin to appear in the movie *From Justin to Kelly*, a musical in which the *Idol* contestants play young people on spring break in Miami. The movie cost more to produce than it made at the box office. It was widely panned by critics. Kelly admitted that she could tell from reading the script that the movie was not going to turn out well.

Still, Kelly had no pretensions of being an actress. The closest she had ever come to being on camera as an actress had been during her first stay in Los Angeles when she appeared as an **extra** on a few television programs just to pay her rent. Kelly basically got paid to sit around on the sets of such programs as *Sabrina: The Teenage Witch* and *The Bernie Mac Show*. Now, with little preparation, she was cast as the female lead of a movie.

A reviewer for *Entertainment Weekly* had this to say about *From Justin to Kelly*:

"How bad is From Justin to Kelly? Set in Miami during spring break, it's like *Grease: The Next Generation* acted out by the food-court staff at SeaWorld. Justin, cast as the

cool-dude 'mayor' of spring break, spends the entire movie getting his text messages crossed with nice girl Kelly Clarkson. **"**

Meanwhile a reviewer from the Web site Filmcritic.com wrote that he didn't think any one could have saved the movie.

"The subplots and supporting characters are too lame to even describe, and the musical numbers add nothing to the production. Songs, all of which sound to have been composed on the same Casio keyboard, don't coyly comment or add jazz to the plot. If the songs were on the radio, you'd turn it off. "

American Dreams Role

In 2003, Kelly was offered another dramatic role that was more to her liking and abilities. She was asked to appear on a two-part episode of NBC's *American Dreams*, a program that was notable for using real-life singers to play recording stars from the 1960s. Other singers who made guest appearances on *American Dreams* were Alicia Keys and sisters Hilary and Haylie Duff.

Kelly was cast as Brenda Lee, a pop and country singer who started recording songs when she was a young girl. Dressed in a strapless 1960's era bright yellow gown and wig, Kelly sang one of Lee's hits, "Sweet Nothin's," on the program. Although Kelly was excited to play Lee, she had no idea who the singer was until she asked her mother. Having learned a bit about the singer she played, Kelly concluded that they had some things in common. She said, "She's very cool. She was very rock. She started out doing country and then she got real rock. That was cool."

Touring Around the World

To reach her fans in the U.S. and around the world, Kelly began touring. Her first official tour was with *American Idol* right after

Kelly has another chance at acting as she appears in the role of 1960s singer Brenda Lee on the TV series *American Dreams*. Kelly enjoyed learning more about Brenda's career and sang one of her country hits on the show.

she won the competition; she visited 30 cities with the other top 10 performers. As 2004 dawned she again visited 30 cities, this time with Clay Aiken, the second-place finisher on the second season of *Idol*. Kelly and Clay didn't know each other well at first, but when Kelly learned that Clay would be touring she decided it would be fun to go together. She discovered that Clay was a simple person like her who was willing to pass the time on the tour bus playing Scrabble. Kelly resisted all attempts by anyone who tried to treat her like a star. Her onstage wardrobe choices were nothing fancy. She recalled,

> **"My ritual of getting up every day is I wake up on the bus, I'll slip my contacts in, I'll put the makeup and hair on with my makeup artist, then I'll put my jeans and shirt on and go onstage."**

World Idol Competition

Kelly also competed in one last *Idol* event, this time in a competition known as *World Idol*. She flew to London to match her singing talents against those of others who won similar competitions in 10 other countries in which versions of *Idol* appear: Australia, Great Britain, Germany, Belgium, Holland, Canada, Poland, South Africa, Lebanon, and Norway.

Oddsmakers predicted Kelly would win the contest or, if she did not, that British *Idol* winner Will Young would take the prize. But neither won the competition, which involved singing in front of an international panel of judges as viewers voted for the contestant of their choice. Simon served as the U.S. judge. Kelly sang Aretha Franklin's "(You Make Me Feel Like) A Natural Woman" in a performance that led to her being voted the second-place finisher.

She was beaten by the *Norwegian Idol*, Kurt Nilsen, a 25-year-old former plumber who sings with a band called Fenrik Lane. Nilsen performed "Beautiful Day," a U2 composition, winning despite unkind comments made by the judge from Australia, who compared him to a character from *Lord of the Rings*. The judge said, "You have the voice of an angel and the face of a Hobbit."

Second Album

As Kelly fulfilled her other obligations she also continued writing songs for her second album, *Breakaway*, which became a top-selling album in 2005 and the one for which she won two Grammys.

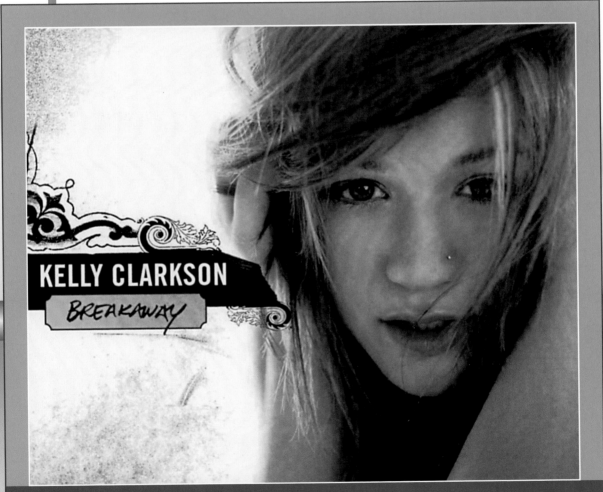

Kelly's second album, *Breakaway*, shot to the top of the charts in 2005. Kelly wrote or co-wrote half the album's songs, including the Grammy-winning "Since U Been Gone." She also shot a music video of the song, which won an MTV Video Music Award.

Kelly belts out a song at the 2005 NBA All-Star Game. Kerry's life after *Idol* was incredibly busy. Her album sales and rising fame led to TV appearances, such as *Saturday Night Live* and *The Oprah Winfrey Show*, commercials, and product endorsements.

One of the Grammys was for "Since U Been Gone," a song *Blender* magazine placed in the top 100 in a feature story on the greatest 500 songs in recent years. The song also ranked among a select few to sell more than a million copies as digital downloads.

Kelly wrote or co-wrote half the tracks on the album, which sold more than 10 million copies. She was credited with writing "Behind These Hazel Eyes," "Because of You," "Addicted," "Where is Your Heart," "Walk Away," and "Hear Me." The Avril Lavigne–penned title track song "Breakaway" sung by Kelly was featured in the movie *The Princess Diaries 2: Royal Engagement*, while "Since U Been Gone" can be found on the video game *Dance Dance Revolution SuperNOVA*. Kelly's video for "Since U Been Gone," in which the singer trashes her boyfriend's apartment, won an MTV Award for best pop video and best female video. A reviewer for *Time* had this to say about *Breakaway*:

> **❝She works with strong producers, picks crisp, up-tempo songs that mine a slender emotional vein (to summarize: Why did you leave me, you jerk?) and sings them with an understatement alien to most of her peers. It's an (almost) guiltless pleasure.❞**

To help promote the album, Kelly performed on *Saturday Night Live*, singing two songs from the album. She also made an appearance on Oprah Winfrey's popular daytime program. Her newfound popularity also gave her the opportunity to sign some product endorsement deals, becoming a familiar face on advertisements for Candies shoes and working out a deal with the Ford Motor Company allowing the automaker to use her song "Go" in its commercials.

Fighting for Her Beliefs

Although Kelly said she was "100 percent happy" with the album, her desire to include so many of her own songs was not supported by her record company. She resented recording executives telling her she did not know her own audience as well as they did. She especially did not like being told she did not know how to write pop music. She recalled,

Kelly visits Bangkok, Thailand, before the 2005 MTV Asia Aid tsunami relief concert. Kelly used her newfound celebrity to help others in many ways. She became a Team Youth Ambassador for the March of Dimes and supported Musicians on Call.

> **"They hated 'Miss Independent' on my first album. It was No. 1 for six weeks, then they got behind it. They hated 'Breakaway.' The song they hated the most was 'Because of You.' I fought and fought for it, it became successful, and they finally got behind it."**

As a result of this friction Kelly decided to end her relationship with 19 Entertainment, the management company associated with *American Idol*. She phoned 19 Entertainment head Simon Fuller about her decision shortly after New Year's Day, 2004. Kelly retained a new manager, then took some time off to relax after working virtually nonstop since her *American Idol* audition.

With more money than she had ever had in her life, Kelly treated her mother to a new house and began thinking about using her celebrity status to make a difference in other people's lives. Kelly became the celebrity Team Youth Ambassador for the March of Dimes and began contributing personal possessions to be auctioned by Musicians on Call, a nonprofit group that brings music to hospital patients. In addition, Kelly took part in a benefit to raise money for victims of the 2004 tsunami in the Indian Ocean that devastated many Asian and African countries.

RAISING MONEY FOR TSUNAMI VICTIMS

In December 2004, an earthquake and giant wave of water known as a tsunami struck parts of Asia and Africa, wiping out hundreds of thousands of lives and destroying portions of eight countries.

Many people were moved to donate money to help the tsunami victims rebuild their lives. Kelly was one of those celebrities who participated in an MTV Asia Aid Benefit concert in Bangkok, Thailand, in February 2005. Money raised from the concert directly benefited UNICEF (United Nations Children's Fund) and other relief organizations in Thailand and India. Other performers were Jennifer Lopez, Sting, 50 Cent, Ricky Martin, Moby, and Ronan Keating, as well as the bands Good Charlotte, Green Day, and Hoobastank.

A glamorous Kelly proudly holds her award for Favorite Female Performer at the 2006 People's Choice Awards. Kelly continued to be amazed by her growing success. Her life seemed to be a fairytale story come true.

5

Living a Cinderella Story

Kelly is a songwriter who mines her own life experiences for song lyrics. Many of the songs Kelly has composed are about disappointment in love—a subject that is certainly common enough in pop songs. Too busy to date someone seriously, Kelly admits to having had several good relationships with men and only one that involved a bad breakup.

It is that relationship that she turns to for inspiration for her "bad break up songs" like "Never Again." Kelly is certain that the young man who treated her poorly knows that those songs are about him, but this doesn't bother her. And she says she actually likes being single because dating is hard work.

Sometimes, though, the songs she crafts seem like they are about romantic relationships when they are not. Such was the case with her song "Cry," from her fourth album, *All I Ever Wanted*. That song was based on the hurt Kelly experienced from the loss of a friendship with a girlfriend.

Music Keeps Her Awake

While some writers suffer from writer's block, the inability to find the words they need to express themselves, Kelly may have the opposite problem. She admits to having song ideas pop into her head just about everywhere. She uses a laptop computer with software that lets her record songs at any time—even when she is in bed—and has a BlackBerry to keep track of her ideas while she away from home. Before obtaining the BlackBerry, which allows her to record text messages, she had to jot down ideas and lyrics on pieces of scrap paper, such as napkins she'd find in restaurants. She says,

“Sometimes I wake up at four in the morning, my head spinning with ideas, and I grab the laptop, which is always besides me. I'm on my third laptop since I bought the bed. The first two fell off the side and broke.”

It was Kelly's insistence on writing her own lyrics that led to an all-out tug-of-war over her third album, *My December*, released in the summer of 2007. This time the gutsy singer-songwriter took on Clive Davis, head of a major record company, Sony BMG. Davis, who is in his seventies, is a giant in the industry who has worked with Whitney Houston, Aretha Franklin, and Justin Timberlake.

Personal Vision

Kelly's vision for *My December* was more personal and included more rock 'n' roll music than her first two albums. This time, she wanted to produce an album composed entirely of her own songs

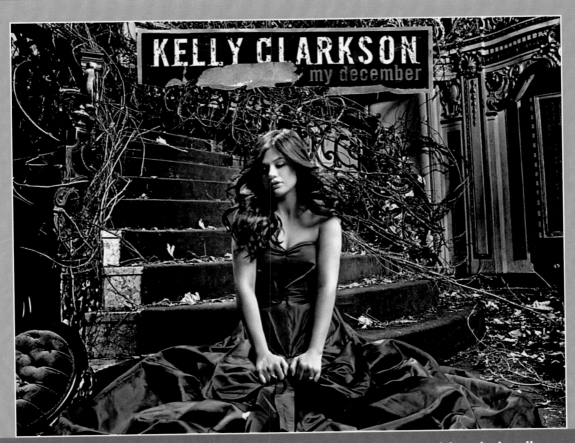

Kelly's album *My December* contained more of her own music. Although the album was not a smash, Simon said, "Kelly will be here for 30 years. She has one of the best pop voices in the world right now. . . . She's not a girl who got lucky in a talent competition; we got lucky to find her."

and focusing on some of the disappointments she had experienced in the past two years.

She wanted to prove she could stand on her own instead of relying on the proven track record of the hit-makers with whom Davis had paired her in the past. But Davis, who was concerned about whether the album Kelly envisioned would make money, protested that the album would not produce a single hit song. He delayed the album's release but eventually gave in to Kelly's demands. Kelly said,

> **"I know it's not going to do what *Breakaway* did, [because] it's not as mainstream. I get that. Some of the songs are not what 10-year-olds are probably going to listen to. But we all go through situations for certain reasons, and I think we should share that. This record is more intense, it's more raw, it's more emotional. But it's not *that* different. It's not Metallica. Even if it does tank—who cares? It's one album. "**

No Pushover

In the end, Davis proved to be right about *My December*'s commercial appeal; the album sold 2.5 million copies, far less than *Breakaway*. Still, Kelly had no regrets. The one hit song from *My December*, "Never Again," channeled the ugly emotions she felt after her boyfriend broke up with her only to announce that he was marrying someone else. Kelly was happy with the album and proud of herself for standing up to her record company. She said,

> **"I can't stand it when people put out the same record over and over again. It's annoying. If you're going with the flow and not fighting, that's settling. I can't take that. Life is just too short to be a pushover. "**

Record reviews for *My December* were not all bad. *Entertainment Weekly* wrote,

> **"Where Clarkson hits us with her best shot is in the confessionals in which she ditches the blame game and draws her own blood. . . . Clarkson's most vulnerable moments are accomplished and affecting—from the frisky pleadings of 'Can I Have a Kiss' to the near-suicidal despair of 'Irvine.' "**

Going Country

One consequence of the heated battle over *My December* was that Kelly had to cancel a high-priced summer arena tour due to poor ticket sales. Instead, Kelly scheduled a smaller tour to promote *My December*. She also decided to switch management firms for the second time; once again she felt as though her representatives were not in her corner.

This time Kelly signed with a firm run by country singer Reba McEntire's husband, Narvel Blackstock. Kelly had been a long-time fan of Reba's, having grown up listening to the country and

Reba McEntire (left) and Kelly perform a country version of "Because of You" at the 2007 Academy of Country Music Awards. As a girl, Kelly was influenced by country music and had posters of Reba on her walls. The two later worked together in the 2 Worlds 2 Voices Tour.

western star's music. As a young girl, Kelly hung posters of Reba on her bedroom walls. In 2007, Reba and Kelly recorded a country version of "Because of You" for Reba's album *Duets* that rocketed to second place on *Billboard* magazine's Hot Country Chart. The two artists were nominated for a Best Country Collaboration with Vocals Award at the Academy of Country Music Awards in 2008, and also performed the song during the Academy's nationally televised awards show. Reba and Kelly also collaborated on a *Country Music Television Crossroads* special. The two singers toured together in a series of shows titled the 2 Worlds 2 Voices Tour.

Kelly has said that someday she hopes to record a country album, and indeed country music has been a big influence on her singing style. *Blender* magazine touched on that influence when it described her voice:

> **"The Texas native has one of the great voices in pop music, a powerful and versatile instrument that's steeped in the rhythm and blues and country music she grew up with in the South. If Mariah Carey's five octave voice is the equivalent of an expensively bred poodle, then Clarkson's is a bloodhound: friendly, earthy, but fierce just the same."**

NASCAR Ambassador

In addition to touring with Reba, Kelly also got to live another Texas girlhood fantasy—hurtling around the Daytona International Speedway racetrack in Florida at breakneck speed in a car with NASCAR racing driver Jimmie Johnson. Kelly got the opportunity as a perk of being named a NASCAR ambassador in 2007. Earlier she had served as a grand marshal at the Auto Club Speedway in Fontana, California. Kelly, who comes from a family of racing fans, was in her country glory. In fact, some people were expecting that her next album would be a country album. But with her fourth effort, *All I Ever Wanted*, she once again collaborated with

Kelly is in her country glory as she climbs out of the pace car at the NASCAR Nextel Cup Series Sony HD 500 in 2006. As a NASCAR ambassador, she got to live her fantasy of riding in a fast car around a famous racetrack.

the team that made her early hits and returned to the top of the charts in 2009.

Entertainment Weekly, which named Kelly its "Entertainer of the Month" that March, said, "With her new album *All I Ever Wanted* debuting at No. 1 on *Billboard*'s charts and nabbing the second biggest opening week sales of 2009, Clarkson has re-established herself as a pop music princess—and one of the few *American Idol* winners who can still deliver a blockbuster." Her single "My Life Would Suck Without You" became Kelly's second No. 1 hit and set a record for the greatest ratings jump after it zoomed from No. 97 to No. 1 on *Billboard*'s Hot 100. The *Washington Post*'s review said,

> 66 'My Life Would Suck Without You'. . . is a nearly perfect example of slick, carefully crafted 21st-century pop. The melody is Krazy Glue-sticky, the production super-compressed, the arrangement airtight. 99

The seven winners of *American Idol*, (from left) Ruben, Kelly, Fantasia, David, Carrie, Taylor, and Jordin, hold silver microphone awards as they attend the 2009 grand opening of the American Idol Experience attraction at Walt Disney World. That was a great year for Kelly as her new album got rave reviews and debuted at No. 1 on the charts.

In 2009, Kelly was one of the *Idol* stars who helped open the American Idol Experience attraction at Walt Disney World Resort in Florida. *Idol* winners from each season all participated. The attraction gives guests an opportunity to get the feel of *Idol*, auditioning before judges and performing in front of audience members who vote for the top performer of the day. The winner is rewarded with an opportunity to audition in front of *American Idol* producers.

As songs from her fourth album stayed at the top of the charts, Kelly was invited to perform the national anthem at the opening of the new Yankee Stadium in New York City in the spring of 2009. It was one of the most spectacular events of Kelly's career—while she sang, four U.S. Air Force F-16 Fighting Falcon jets flew overhead.

Still Kelly

While a lot has happened in Kelly's life in a few short years, she believes she has not changed much at all. "My central foundation is my faith. That's just how I keep it, like sane," she said. Meanwhile, she still lives in Texas, only now in a home that sits on a 50-acre property that includes a go-kart track. She likes to hang out at home with her brother Jason, who lives with her. Kelly is famous enough that going out in public can be difficult. Becasue she spends so much time touring, she cherishes her quiet time home alone playing *Guitar Hero*, skeet shooting, or simply relaxing.

Now wealthy, Kelly has the luxury of giving back to her fans and favorite causes. One of her favorite charities is the Susan G. Komen Breast Cancer Foundation, to which she donated a portion of the proceeds from her *Addicted* tour to promote her *Breakaway* album. She is also concerned about stopping **global warming** and in 2007 performed in the Live Earth concert staged at Giants Stadium in East Rutherford, New Jersey. Live Earth included a series of concerts staged across the globe to raise awareness about climate change.

March 23, 2009

CASHBOX
magazine, inc ®™

KELLY CLARKSON ®™

MY LIFE WOULD SUCK WITHOUT YOU

THE TOP
MUSIC CHARTS
MUSIC NEWS
CD REVIEWS
INDIE ARTISTS
CELEBRITY INTERVIEWS
STREAMING RADIO
MORE AND...

#1 CASHBOX
Preformed medley on OPRAH
"Because of You,"
"Behind These Hazel Eyes," and
"My Life Would Suck Without You"

Although she now appears on magazine covers and concert stages countrywide, Kelly still thinks of herself as a small-town girl. She is firmly rooted in Texas, with her family nearby. At the same time, she reaches for the stars and continues to fulfill her seemingly limitless potential.

Friend of the Environment

In July 2007, Kelly participated in a large outdoor concert at Giants Stadium as part of the international Live Earth effort to increase public awareness about global warming. The event also helped raise funds for the Alliance for Climate Protection and other environmental organizations.

Also on the bill for the Giants Stadium concert were Kanye West, Fall Out Boy, AFI, Akon, Ludacris, Rihanna, Smashing Pumpkins, The Police, Bon Jovi, Dave Matthews Band, Roger Waters, Alicia Keys, Faith Hill, Tim McGraw, John Mayer, KT Tunstall, and Melissa Etheridge.

The concert was one of seven international concerts organized by former vice president Al Gore and other environmental activists that took place that day.

American Idol Lives On

Another thing that has not changed is that she still has a place in her life for the TV show *American Idol,* which Kelly watches when she has the time. She dismissed accusations that suggest she prefers to think she did not get her start on the program. She said,

> **People have the wrong idea, like I don't want to talk about it. I think it's a great thing. It was obviously the best way for me to come into the business and it's just like a great opportunity for everyday normal people. It's like a Cinderella story every day.**

1982 Kelly Brianne Clarkson born on April 24 in Fort Worth, Texas.

1988 Parents separate.

1991 Mother remarries.

1997 Turns down first record contract.

2000 Graduates from Burleson High School and moves to Los Angeles.

2001 Enters *American Idol* competition.

2002 After months of competing against other singers, wins the first *American Idol* competition.

2003 First single, "A Moment Like This," released.

First album, *Thankful*, released.

2004 *Breakaway* released.

2005 Named *Blender* magazine's Woman of the Year.

2006 Wins Grammy awards for Best Female Pop Vocal Performance and Best Pop Vocal Album.

2007 Participates in Live Earth Concert.

Third album, *My December*, released.

2008 Teams up with Reba McEntire in 2 Worlds 2 Voices Tour.

2009 Opens Disney's American Idol Experience in Disney World.

Fourth album, *All I Ever Wanted*, released.

Awards and Nominations

2002 Wins Billboard Music Award for Best Selling Single of the Year for "A Moment Like This."

2003 Nominated for MTV Video Music Award, Best New Artist, for "Miss Independent"; wins Teen Choice Award for Choice Music Female Artist.

2004 Nominated for Grammy Award, Best Female Pop Vocal Performance, for "Miss Independent."

2005 Wins American Music Awards for Artist of the Year and Favorite Adult Contemporary Artist and MTV Video Music Award for Best Female Video; nominated for Viewer's Choice Award for "Since U Been Gone." Wins Teen Choice Awards: Choice Music Album for *Breakaway*; Choice Music Female Artist; Choice Music Single for "Since U Been Gone"; and Choice Summer Song for "Behind These Hazel Eyes." Nominated for World Music Award for World's Best-Selling Pop Female Artist.

2006 Wins Grammy Awards for Best Female Pop Vocal Performance for "Since U Been Gone" and Best Pop Vocal Album for *Breakaway*; MTV Video Music Award for Best Female Video, "Because of You"; Blip Award for Favorite Female Singer; Nickelodeon Kids' Choice Award, People's Choice Award for Favorite Female Performer, and Teen Choice Award for Choice Music—Female Artist.

2007 Wins ASCAP Pop Music Award for Song of the Year, "Because of You."

2008 Nominated for Academy of Country Music Award, Vocal Event of the Year, for "Because of You," and nominated for Grammy Award for Best Country Collaboration with Vocals for "Because of You," with Reba McEntire and nominated for Academy of Country Music Best Country Collaboration, with Reba McEntire.

Albums

2003 *Thankful*

2004 *Breakaway*

2007 *My December*

2009 *All I Ever Wanted*

Films

2003 *From Justin to Kelly*

ballad—Style of song that tells a complete story.

bar mitzvah—Coming of age ceremony in the Jewish religion for 13-year-old boys.

bulimic—Having an eating disorder in which a person purposely vomits to prevent weight gain.

choreography—Rehearsed dance steps often coordinated with others.

comeback—Attempt by a recording artist who has fallen out of popularity to regain his or her former status.

extra—Actor hired to appear in scenes of a television show or movie, usually as part of a crowd, but given no lines to speak.

global warming—Increase in the world's temperatures, believed to be caused in part by higher levels of carbon dioxide in the atmosphere.

karaoke—Originating in Japan, a popular form of entertainment in which people sing words to well-known songs using recorded musical accompaniments.

platinum—Designation achieved when a record sells at least one million copies.

Books and Periodicals

Cowell, Simon. *I Don't Mean to Be Rude, But . . .: Backstage Gossip from American Idol & the Secrets that Can Make You a Star.* New York: Broadway Books, 2003.

Downey, Laura. "Kelly Clarkson: The Original American Idol Talks About Beating Clay Aiken at Scrabble and Making the Most of Their Road Trip," *People* (March 26, 2004): www.people.com/people/article/0,,628463,00.html.

Gardner, Elysa. "Clarkson's 'Thankful' Much Obliged to Many," *USA Today* (April 4, 2003): www.usatoday.com/life/music/reviews/2003-04-14-kelly_x.htm.

Henry, Denise. "Kelly Clarkson," *Scholastic Action* (October 9, 2006): p. 4.

Hollandsworth, Skip. "Since She's Been Gone," *Texas Monthly* (May 2005): www.texasmonthly.com/2005-05-01/feature.php.

Tracy, Kathleen. *Kelly Clarkson.* Hockessin, Delaware: Mitchell Lane Publishers, 2007.

Tryangiel, Josh. "Miss Independent: How Kelly Clarkson Shed Her 'Idol' Crown and Stole Pop Music's Throne." *Time* (February 13, 2006): p. 68.

Walsh, Marissa. *American Idol: The Search for a Superstar.* New York: Bantam Books, 2002.

Web Sites

www.americanidol.com

American Idol's official Web site includes information on the current season's contestants, including episode recaps and information about American Idol's charity, Idol Gives Back.

www.grammy.com

Official site of the Grammy Awards has videos and still photos from past award shows, information about the Grammy Museum in Los Angeles and is searchable for past winners.

www.kellyclarkson.com

Official Web site for Kelly Clarkson has information on her fan club and tour schedule as well as music and lyrics from all of her albums.

www.musiciansoncall.org

The Web site for nonprofit group Musicians On Call provides live and recorded music for hospital patients to help them heal. Items donated by musicians that are up for auction can be viewed.

page

ABOUT THE AUTHOR

Gail Snyder is a freelance writer and advertising copywriter who has written more than 15 books for young readers. She lives in Chalfont, Pennsylvania, with her husband Hal, and daughter Ashley, not far from where Justin Guarini grew up.